EASTER JOKES BOOK

IF YOU LAUGH, YOU LOSE

EASTER JOKES GAME RULES

PICK YOUR TEAM, OR GO ONE ON ONE.

SIT ACROSS FROM EACH OTHER AND MAKE EYE CONTACT.

TAKE TURNS READING JOKES TO EACH OTHER.

YOU CAN MAKE SILLY FACES, FUNNY SOUND EFFECTS, ETC.

WHEN YOUR OPPONENT LAUGHS, YOU GET A POINT.

FIRST TEAM TO WIN MORE POINTS BY THE END OF THE GAME, **WINS.**

if you laugh, you lose

HOW DO YOU CATCH A RABBIT?

Make a noise like a carrot.

WHAT DO YOU GET IF YOU POUR BOILING HOT WATER DOWN A RABBIT HOLE?

Hot cross bunnies.

WHERE DOES A BUNNY GO IF YOU GIVE IT A PAIR OF SOCKS?

A sock hop.

WHAT DID THE EASTER BUNNY SAY TO THE CARROT?

"It's been nice gnawing you!"

HOW DOES THE EASTER BUNNY PAINT ALL THE EASTER EGGS?

He hires Santa's elves during the off season.

WHERE DOES THE EASTER BUNNY EAT BREAKFAST?

IHOP.

HOW DO RABBITS TRAVEL?

By HAREplanes.

HOW DID THE RABBIT CROSS THE ROAD?

He hopped he could.

WHAT KIND OF STORIES DO RABBITS LIKE BEST?

Ones with hoppy endings.

WHAT DO YOU GET WHEN YOU CROSS A RABBIT WITH AN OYSTER?

The oyster bunny.

HOW DO YOU KILL A UNIQUE RABBIT?

You neak up on it.

WHAT DID THE FATHER EASTER EGG DO WHEN THE MOTHER EASTER EGG TOLD HIM A JOKE?

He cracked up!

WHY DO RABBITS EAT CARROTS?

Because they don't want to be nearsighted!

WHAT DOES A BUNNY RABBIT DO IN THE RAIN?

Get wet!

WHAT KIND OF MUSIC DO BUNNIES LIKE?

Hip Hop.

WHAT DO BUNNIES DO WHEN THEY GET MARRIED?

Go on a bunnymoon!

HOW DOES A RABBIT THROW A TANTRUM?

He gets hopping mad.

WHAT STORIES DOES THE EASTER BUNNY LIKE BEST?

The ones with happy eggings!

WHAT DO YOU GET IF YOU CROSS A BEE AND A BUNNY?

A honey bunny!

WHAT DOES THE EASTER BUNNY SAY WHEN IT BURPS?

"Eggs-cuse me!"

HOW DO YOU KNOW
CARROTS ARE GOOD FOR
YOUR EYES?

Have you ever seen
a rabbit wearing glasses?!

WHAT HAPPENED TO THE
EASTER EGG WHEN IT
HEARD A FUNNY JOKE?

It cracked up!

WHY DON'T YOU SEE DINOSAURS AT EASTER?

Because they are eggs-tinct!

HOW CAN YOU TELL WHERE THE EASTER BUNNY HAS BEEN?

Eggs mark the spot!

HOW DOES EASTER END?

With an R!

HOW DID THE EASTER BUNNY RATE HIS FAVOURITE RESTAURANT?

Egg-cellent!

WHAT DO YOU CALL AN EASTER EGG FROM OUTER SPACE?

An Egg-stra-terrestrial!

WHAT HAPPENED TO THE EASTER BUNNY WHEN HE WAS NAUGHTY AT SCHOOL?

He was eggs-pelled!

WHY IS THE EASTER BUNNY SO SMART?

He's an egghead.

WHAT KIND OF BUNNY CAN'T HOP?

Ones made of chocolate!

WHY DO WE PAINT EASTER EGGS?

Because it's easier than wallpapering th

CHRISTMAS DOES COME BEFORE EASTER IN ONE PLACE—BUT WHERE?

The dictionary!

WHAT'S THE BEST WAY TO MAKE EASTER EASIER?

Put an "i" where the "t" is.

WHERE DOES EASTER TAKE PLACE EVERY YEAR?

Where eggs marks the spot!

HOW DOES EASTER END?

With an "R"!

WHAT SHOULD YOU DO TO PREPARE FOR ALL THE EASTER TREATS?

Eggs-ercise!

HOW CAN YOU MAKE EASTER PREPARATIONS GO FASTER?

Use the eggs-press lane!

WHAT KIND OF BEAN CAN'T GROW IN A GARDEN?

A jelly bean.

WHAT KIND OF JEWELRY IS THE BEST EASTER GIFT?

A 14-carrot gold necklace.

WHAT DO YOU CALL A RABBIT WITH FLEAS?

Bugs Bunny.

WHAT DO YOU GET IF YOU GIVE AN EASTER BUNNY A PAIR OF SOCKS?

A sock hop!

WHY WAS THE EASTER BUNNY SO SAD?

He was having a bad hare day.

HOW DOES AN EASTER BUNNY KEEP HIS FUR LOOKING SO GOOD?

Hare spray.

HOW DOES THE EASTER BUNNY STAY FIT?

Hare-obics.

HOW DO YOU WRITE A LETTER TO AN EASTER BUNNY?

Use hare-mail!

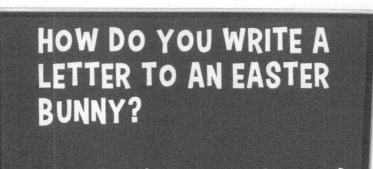

WHAT THE EASTER BUNNY'S FAVORITE DANCE MOVE?

The bunny hop.

WHAT DO YOU CALL AN EASTER BUNNY WITH A BAD MEMORY?

A hare-brain!

WHAT'S THE EASTER BUNNY'S FAVORITE SPORT?

Basket-ball.

WHAT KIND OF RABBIT TELLS JOKES?

A funny bunny.

WHY DID THE EASTER EGG HIDE?

It was a little chicken.

WHAT DID THE EASTER EGG ASK FOR AT THE HAIR SALON?

A new dye-job.

WHAT HAPPENS IF YOU TELL A JOKE TO AN EASTER EGG?

It cracks up.

WHAT'S AN EASTER EGG'S LEAST FAVORITE DAY?

Fry-day.

WHAT DO YOU CALL A VERY TIRED EASTER EGG?

Eggs-austed.

WHERE DOES THE EASTER BUNNY GET HIS EGGS?

From an eggplant.

WHAT DO YOU GET IF YOU CROSS WINNIE THE POOH AND THE EASTER BUNNY?

A honey bunny.

HOW MANY CHOCOLATE BUNNIES CAN YOU PUT INTO AN EMPTY EASTER BASKET?

Only one because after that, it's not empty!

HOW DID THE SOGGY EASTER BUNNY DRY HIMSELF?

With a hare dryer!

HOW DO YOU CATCH A TAME RABBIT?

Tame way, unique up on it.

WHAT HAPPENED WHEN THE EASTER BUNNY MET THE RABBIT OF HIS DREAMS?

They lived hoppily ever after!

WHY CAN'T A RABBIT'S NOSE BE TWELVE INCHES LONG?

Because then it would be a foot.

HOW CAN YOU TELL WHICH RABBITS ARE THE OLDEST IN A GROUP?

Just look for the gray hares.

WHAT KIND OF JEWELRY DO RABBITS WEAR?

14 carrot gold.

WHY DID THE EASTER EGG HIDE?

He was a little chicken

HOW DOES A RABBIT MAKE GOLD SOUP?

He begins with 24 carrots.

WHAT DO YOU GET WHEN YOU CROSS A BUNNY WITH A SPIDER?

A harenet.

WHY DOES THE EASTER BUNNY HAVE A SHINY NOSE?

His powder puff is on the wrong end.

WHY IS A BUNNY THE LUCKIEST ANIMAL IN THE WORLD?

It has four rabbits' feet.

WHAT DO YOU GET WHEN YOU CROSS A BUNNY WITH AN ONION?

A bunion.

WHEN IS AN ELEPHANT LIKE THE EASTER BUNNY?

When he's wearing his cute little Easter Bunny suit.

WHY COULDN'T THE RABBIT FLY HOME FOR EASTER?

He didn't have the hare fare.

WHY DID THE RABBIT CROSS THE ROAD?

Because the chicken had his Easter eggs.

WHAT DO YOU CALL A TRANSFORMER BUNNY?

Hop-timus Prime.

WHAT STORIES DO EGGS TELL THEIR CHILDREN?

Yolk tales.

WHY DID HUMPTY DUMPTY HAVE A GREAT FALL?

To make up for his miserable summer.

WHY DID THE JELLY BEAN GO TO SCHOOL?

Because he really wanted to be a Smartie.

WHAT KIND OF VEGETABLE IS ANGRY?

A steamed carrot!

WOULD FEBRUARY MARCH?

No, but April May.

HOW DO EGGS LEAVE THE HIGHWAY?

They went through the eggs-it

WHY DID THE EGG GO TO BED?

Because it was fried.

WHAT CAME FIRST, THE CHICKEN OR THE EGG?

Neither the easter bunny

HOW DO YOU MAKE A RABBIT STEW?

Make it wait a few hours.

WHAT DID THE EGGS DO ON THE INTERNET?

They looked for a good egg-site.

WHAT IS A BUNNY'S FAVORITE KIND OF MOVIE?

The kind with a hoppy ending.

WHY ARE YOU STUDYING YOUR EASTER CANDY?

I'm trying to decide which came first the chocolate chicken or the chocolate egg.

WHY DID THE ROBIN SAVE ALL ITS MONEY?

It wanted a little nest egg someday.

WHAT DO CHICKENS CALL A SCHOOL TEST?

Eggs-amination.

WHERE DO RABBITS GO AFTER THEIR WEDDING?

On their bunny-moon.

WHAT DID THE BUNNY
WANT TO DO WHEN HE
GREW UP?

Join the hare force.

WHERE DO YOU FIND
DINOSAUR PEEPS?

Peep-arassic Park.

WHAT DID THE EGGS DO WHEN THE LIGHT TURNED GREEN?

They egg-celerated.

HOW FAR CAN YOU PUSH A CHICKEN?

Not far, but you can pullet.

WHAT DO BAMBI AND EASTER BUNNY HAVE IN COMMON?

They are both buck-toothed.

WHY DO FARMERS BURY THEIR MONEY IN THE GROUND?

They want to have rich soil.

WHY DID THE ROBIN
SAVE ALL ITS MONEY?

It wanted a little
nest egg someday.

WHY DON'T DINOSAURS
CELEBRATE EASTER?

They're eggs-tinct.

WHY DO BUNNIES LIKE MATH SO MUCH?

They're always multiplying.

WHAT IS THE DIFFERENCE BETWEEN THANKSGIVING AND APRIL FOOLS DAY?

One day you are thankful and the other you are prankful.

WHY DID THE EASTER BUNNY GIVE EGGS TO EVERYBODY?

He doesn't want to put all his eggs in one basket.

WHAT DID THE EASTER BUNNY SAY WHEN HE WAS LEFT TO COLOR ALL THE EGGS BY HIMSELF?

I'm dyeing over here.

WHAT DO YOU GET WHEN YOU CROSS THE EASTER BUNNY AND A FROG?

Rabbit, rabbit, rabbit.

WHY WON'T EASTER EGGS GO OUT AT NIGHT?

They don't want to get "beat up"

WHY DID THE EASTER BUNNY WANT TO BE A COMEDIAN?

He was a funny bunny.

WHY DOES THE EASTER BUNNY ONLY DELIVER ONCE A YEAR?

Hare today, gone tomorrow.

KNOCK KNOCK!
WHO'S THERE?
WENDY.
WENDY WHO?
WENDY EASTER EGG
HUNT GONNA' START?

KNOCK, KNOCK
WHO'S THERE?
EASTER
EASTER WHO?
THE EASTER BUNNY!

KNOCK, KNOCK
WHO'S THERE?
ANA
ANA WHO?
ANA-OTHER EASTER BUNNY!

KNOCK, KNOCK
WHO'S THERE?
MORA
MORA WHO?
MORA EASTER BUNNIES!

KNOCK, KNOCK
WHO'S THERE?
HOWIE
HOWIE WHO?
HOWIE GONNA GET RID OF ALL THESE EASTER BUNNIES?!

KNOCK KNOCK
WHO'S THERE?
EVEN MORE
EVEN MORE WHO?
EVEN MORE EASTER BUNNIES.

KNOCK KNOCK
WHO'S THERE?
CAR
CAR WHO?
CAR COME AND RUN
OVER THE EASTER BUNNIES.

KNOCK, KNOCK
WHO'S THERE?
SOME BUNNY
SOME BUNNY WHO?
SOME BUNNY HAS BEEN
EATING MY EASTER CANDY!

KNOCK, KNOCK!
WHO'S THERE?
HEIDI.
HEIDI WHO?
HEIDI THE EGGS AROUND
THE HOUSE.

KNOCK, KNOCK!
WHO'S THERE?
ALMA.
ALMA WHO?
ALMA EASTER CANDY
IS GONE!

KNOCK, KNOCK!

WHO'S THERE?

ARTHUR.

ARTHUR WHO?

ARTHUR ANY MORE EASTER EGGS TO DECORATE?

KNOCK, KNOCK!

WHO'S THERE?

POLICE.

POLICE WHO?

POLICE HURRY UP AND FIND ALL THE EGGS.

KNOCK, KNOCK!
WHO'S THERE?
SHERWOOD.
SHERWOOD WHO?
SHERWOOD LIKE TO HAVE
AS MUCH EASTER CANDY AS YOU!

KNOCK, KNOCK!
WHO'S THERE?
BOO.
BOO WHO?
DON'T CRY, EASTER WILL
BE BACK NEXT YEAR!

KNOCK, KNOCK!
WHO'S THERE?
BUTCHER.
BUTCHER WHO?
BUTCHER EGGS IN ONE
BASKET!

ONCE THERE WERE TWO
CHOCOLATE BUNNIES AND
ONE HAD THEIR EAR BIT
OFF. ONE SAID, "HAPPY
EASTER."
"HUH?" SAID THE OTHER.

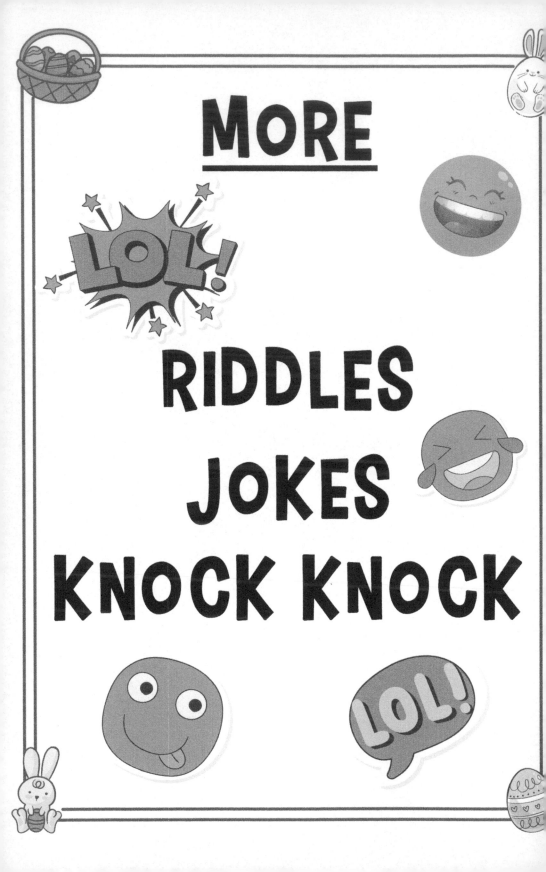

MORE

RIDDLES

JOKES

KNOCK KNOCK

WHY DID THE BANANA GO TO THE DOCTOR'S OFFICE?

BECAUSE HE WASN'T PEELING WELL!

WHY DID THE BEE FEEL COLD?

BECAUSE IT IS IN THE MIDDLE OF A AND C.

WHAT DO YOU DO WHEN YOUR FISH SINGS FLAT?

TUNA FISH!

WHAT DID THE 0 SAY TO THE 8?

"NICE BELT."

WHAT IS THE BIGGEST WORD IN THE WORLD?

SMILES. THERE IS A MILE IN BETWEEN EACH S.

WHAT LETTER IS A DRINK?

T.

WHAT IS GREY, HAS A TAIL AND A TRUNK?

A MOUSE GOING ON A VACATION.

WHAT LETTER IS AN EXCLAMATION?

O!

WHAT DID THE BOY VOLCANO SAY TO THE GIRL VOLCANO?

"I LAVA YOU!"

WHAT DO YOU CALL A DOOR THAT IS CUTE?

ADOORABLE!

TEACHER: HOW MANY SECONDS IN A MINUTE?
STUDENT: 60
TEACHER: HOW MANY MINUTES IN AN HOUR?
STUDENT: 60
TEACHER: GOOD, NOW FOR A HARD ONE, HOW MANY SECONDS IN A YEAR?
STUDENT: 12
TEACHER: 12?
STUDENT: YES, JANUARY 2ND, FEBRUARY 2ND, MARCH 2ND...

THE MOON GOES TO THE HAIR DRESSER.
THE MOON SITS DOWN AND THE SUN
COMES TO DO HIS HAIR. THE SUN SAYS
TO THE MOON, "BEFORE I START ON
YOUR HAIR, DO YOU HAVE ANY-CLIPS?"

TWO MEN WALKED INTO A BAR.
ONE DUCKED AND THE OTHER SAID,
"OUCH!"

MARY HAD A LITTLE LAMB,
BUT THE LAMB STARTED TO TEASE HER.
MARY SAID, "STOP!"
BUT THE LAMB REFUSED
SO NOW IT'S IN THE FREEZER.

IF PIGS COULD FLY, IMAGINE WHAT
THEIR WINGS WOULD TASTE LIKE!

STUDENT ASKING HIS TEACHER: DO YOU PUNISH PEOPLE FOR THINGS THEY DON'T DO?

TEACHER: NO.

STUDENT: GOOD, BECAUSE I HAVEN'T DONE MY HOMEWORK TODAY.

WHEN MY BROTHER TOLD ME TO STOP IMPERSONATING A FLAMINGO I HAD TO PUT MY FOOT DOWN.

PATIENT: DOCTOR, DOCTOR, I'M GOING TO DIE IN 59 SECONDS!
DOCTOR: HANG ON, I'LL BE THERE IN A MINUTE.

DENTIST: STOP MAKING A FACE, I HAVEN'T EVEN TOUCHED YOUR TEETH .
TOMMY: I KNOW, BUT YOU'RE STEPPING ON MY FOOT!

KNOCK, KNOCK
WHO'S THERE?
SCOLD
SCOLD WHO?
SCOLD OUTSIDE!

KNOCK, KNOCK
WHO'S THERE?
WATER
WATER WHO?
WATER YOU DOING IN MY HOUSE!?

KNOCK, KNOCK
WHO'S THERE?
NANA
NANA WHO?
NANA YOUR BUSINESS!

KNOCK, KNOCK
WHO'S THERE?
TENNIS
TENNIS WHO?
TENNIS IS FIVE PLUS FIVE!

KNOCK, KNOCK
WHO'S THERE?
PENCIL
PENCIL WHO?
PENCIL FALL DOWN IF YOU DON'T
WEAR A BELT.

KNOCK, KNOCK
WHO'S THERE?
ZEE
ZEE WHO?
CAN'T YOU ZEE I'M KNOCKING?!

Made in United States
Orlando, FL
10 April 2022

16691862R00050